Happy cooking!

Enjoy!

♡ Sydne

© Sydne George 2016

Print ISBN: 978-1-48357-828-6

eBook ISBN: 978-1-48357-829-3

Little
Red Book of
Recipes to
Love ♥

SYNE GEORGE

$Dear$ Little Red Book of Recipes to Love reader,

Thank you for taking the time to read my cookbook.

I have loved creating in the kitchen for as long as I can remember. I grew up on the kitchen counter watching my beautiful mom whip up everything under the sun for our family. I will be forever grateful to her for sharing her love of cooking and creativity with me.

It has been a labor of love pulling together this collection of favorite recipes that I have enjoyed making again and again for family and friends. These are the go-to tried-and-true recipes I turn to, and what a gift it is to have them all in one place.

My hope is that you will find joy in perusing the pages, and spread the love by cooking recipes from my book for the loved ones in your life.

Recipes are organized by level of difficulty from super simple at the beginning of each section to more time consuming and labor-intensive at the end.

I would love to hear from you if you have comments or questions.

Thanks again.

[signature]

Happy cooking!

• •

Sydne George is a food journalist specializing in recipe development, food writing and food photography. Email her at sydnegeorge@hotmail.com. Sydne's recipes are archived at sydnegeorge.com.

Table of Contents

What a
Wonderful Way
to Start the Day!

Breakfast and Brunch Recipes · · · · · · · · ·

Confetti Eggs • Baked Steel Cut Oatmeal with Apples, Cinnamon and Walnuts

Asparagus, Brie and Chive Tart • Cheesy Ham and Red Potato Strudel • Bagel Bar

Breakfast Crepes with Lingonberry Butter

Confetti Eggs

Who doesn't love a party on their plate first thing in the morning?

Makes two, can be doubled

Make the Confetti Corn, Pepper and Black Bean Sauté:

- 1 tablespoon extra virgin olive oil
- 1 clove garlic, minced
- ¼ cup fresh corn (from an ear of corn on the cob)
- ½ cup diced yellow bell pepper
- ½ cup diced orange bell pepper
- ½ cup diced red bell pepper
- ¼ teaspoon. chili powder
- 1/8 teaspoon cumin
- dash of Kosher salt
- ¼ cup black beans, drained and rinsed

Heat olive oil in medium sauté pan over medium high heat.

When oil is hot, add garlic and sauté, stirring constantly until softened.

Add diced peppers and sauté until lightly browned.

Add remaining ingredients, stirring to combine, just until warmed through.

To assemble:

Poach 2 eggs in salted simmering water to desired degree of doneness.

Remove poached eggs from water and drain on paper towels.

Spoon **Confetti Corn, Pepper and Black Bean Sauté** onto two serving plates.

Top each with poached egg.

Sprinkle with Kosher salt and chili powder.

Top with diced avocado and cilantro sprig.

Enjoy!

Baked Steel Cut Oatmeal with Cinnamon, Apples and Walnuts

Love is in the air, or is that the smell of warm cinnamony-sweet goodness coming from the oven?

Makes a 9 x 13 inch pan

- 3 tablespoon butter
- 2 cups steel-cut oats
- 4 cups water
- 2 teaspoons cinnamon
- 1 teaspoon salt
- ½ cup brown sugar
- 2 ½ cups milk
- 1 teaspoon vanilla
- 1 cup walnuts, coarsely chopped
- 2 cups apples, chopped

Preheat oven to 375 degrees. Butter a 9 x 13 inch baking pan.

Melt butter in a medium sauté pan over medium heat.

Add steel-cut oats to melted butter and toast oats, stirring occasionally. Remove from heat.

Bring water, cinnamon, salt and brown sugar to a simmer in a large cooking pot. Add toasted steel-cut oats and simmer briefly.

Remove from heat.

Add vanilla, walnuts and apples. Stir to combine.

Transfer mixture to greased baking pan.

Bake in upper middle of oven for 1 hour.

Remove from oven.

Spoon into serving bowls and serve with a drizzle of cream.

Enjoy!

Asparagus, Brie and Chive Tart

The go-to guest breakfast you'll love making (and serving and eating!) again and again…

Makes one 9-inch tart

- 1 pound fresh asparagus, stalks washed and trimmed to about 4 inches

For the **crust:**

- 2 cups flour
- ¾ cup vegetable oil
- ¼ cup cold water
- ½ teaspoon salt

For the **filling**:

- 2 eggs
- ¾ cup milk
- 1 tablespoon Dijon mustard
- ¼ teaspoon salt
- ½ cup brie, trimmed and cut in 2 inch strips
- 2 teaspoons freshly snipped chives

Preheat oven to 425 degrees.

Blanch trimmed asparagus in a pot of boiling salted water for 6 minutes. Immediately drain into a colander filled with ice to stop the cooking.

Combine crust ingredients in a medium mixing bowl and stir to combine. Form dough into a ball and roll out between two sheets of waxed paper making a circle about 11 inches in diameter. Transfer dough into 9-inch tart pan with removable bottom. Trim edges.

Arrange blanched asparagus in prepared crust, creating a spoked wheel pattern with asparagus tips pointing outward. Fit brie slices in between asparagus spears.

Whisk together remaining filling ingredients and fill tart shell, being careful not to drown the asparagus. Bake in preheated oven for about 20 minutes, until brie is golden brown and filling is set. Let cool slightly. Slice and serve warm with chive blossoms, if desired.

Enjoy!

Cheesy Ham and Red Potato Strudel

An easy make-ahead brunch creation: just bake, slice and serve with love.

Makes two strudels, to be sliced and served for 4 to 6 people

- 2 cups baby red potatoes, cut into bite-sized pieces
- 1 cup smoked Gouda cheese, grated
- ½ teaspoon salt
- 1 cup honey ham, diced
- ½ teaspoon. fresh rosemary leaves, minced
- 1 8-ounce roll frozen phyllo dough
- ¼ cup melted butter

Bring salted water to a simmer in a medium pot over medium high heat. Add potatoes and cook just until tender, about 6 minutes. Drain in colander and let cool slightly.

Toss cooked potatoes, cheese, salt, ham and rosemary together in medium bowl until well mixed. Transfer to a covered refrigerator dish and chill until ready to assemble.

When ready to assemble:

Preheat oven to 375 degrees.

Unroll 4 sheets of thawed phyllo. Brush with butter.

Top with half of the cheesy ham and potato filling.

Carefully tuck opposite ends of phyllo in toward the center and roll into a long thin strudel roll, brushing with additional melted butter to seal. Repeat filling and rolling to make a second strudel.

Place assembled streusel rolls on buttered baking sheet and bake in preheated oven for 18-20 minutes, until golden brown and flaky. Remove from oven and let rest briefly. Use a sharp serrated bread knife to slice into 1 inch slices. Serve warm with fresh rosemary sprigs for garnish.

Enjoy!

Bagel Bar

Lay out a beautiful breakfast buffet with something for everyone to love.

Sundried Tomato Cream Cheese

- Serve with smoked turkey, bacon and avocado
- 8 ounces cream cheese, softened
- 2 tablespoons sundried tomato paste
- ¼ teaspoon salt

Beat together all ingredients until thoroughly combined. Cover and refrigerate until ready to serve.

Dilled Cream Cheese

- Serve with smoked salmon, capers, red onions
- 8 ounces cream cheese, softened
- 1 clove garlic, minced
- ½ teaspoon dillweed
- ¼ teaspoon salt

Beat together all ingredients until thoroughly combined. Cover and refrigerate until ready to serve.

Pesto Cream Cheese

- Serve with cucumber slices, chives and sunflower seeds
- 8 ounces cream cheese, softened
- ¼ cup prepared pesto

Beat together all ingredients until thoroughly combined. Cover and refrigerate until ready to serve.

Make ahead tips: Mix up the herbed cream cheeses ahead of time. Cook bacon, let cool and refrigerate. Just before serving: slice avocados, cucumbers and red onions. Toast all of the bagels on a baking sheet under the broiler.

Enjoy!

Breakfast Crepes
with Lingonberry Butter

Add this lovely and foolproof crepe recipe to your go-to recipe repertoire.

Basic Crepe Recipe

Serves about 6

- 1 cup milk
- 3 eggs
- 1 tablespoon pure vanilla extract
- 3 tablespoons. melted butter, cooled
- ¾ cup cornstarch
- Dash of salt
- 1 tablespoon sugar

Add ingredients (in order: liquids first) to blender and blend until well mixed. Let rest briefly.

Heat a crepe pan or small nonstick sauté pan over medium high heat. Brush pan with melted butter.

Carefully pour about 2 tbsp. crepe batter from the blender into the hot pan, swirling the pan so the batter covers the bottom on the pan. Cook until edges begin to lightly brown.

Using table knife, lift an edge of the crepe, carefully lift with both hands and flip it over. Cook the other side of the crepe briefly, about 15 seconds. Remove crepe from pan and layer in between sheets of waxed paper until ready to fill and serve.

Lingonberry Butter

- ½ cup butter, softened
- 2 tablespoons lingonberries (jam/jelly aisle)
- Use electric mixer to beat butter and lingonberries together until well-mixed.

Serve a dollop on lingonberry butter over rolled crepes for breakfast.

Enjoy!

Fast, Fresh
and Fabulous!

• •

Best of California Salad • Layered Antipasto Salad Jars • Grilled Steak and Cherry Tomato
Pasta Salad • Baked Sweet Potato with Garlic Roasted Vegetables
Sesame Slaw with Mushrooms, Broccoli and Almonds
Prosciutto, Fig and Caramelized Onion Flatbread

Best of California Cuisine Salad

Swoon over mixed greens tossed with Lover's Lane Mendocino Mustard Dressing, topped with crisp apple matchsticks, Pointe Reye's Blue Cheese and Livermore Walnuts.

Makes 2 dinner salads

Make the Lover's Lane-Mendocino Mustard Dressing:

In a small jar combine:

- 1 tablespoon Mendocino Hot and Sweet Mustard (or other sweet and spicy mustard)

- 1 tablespoon Lover's Lane Honey (or other honey)

- 1 ½ tablespoons red wine vinegar

- 1 tablespoon olive oil

Shake vigorously until well mixed, stirring, if necessary.

Toss dressing with 2 cups of fresh baby greens until incorporated.

Distribute dressed salad onto two salad plates.

Slice Point Reyes blue cheese and arrange atop salad greens.

Slice Aztec Fuji apple (or other crisp apple) into thin matchsticks with sharp knife.

Arrange atop salad greens.

Sprinkle Livermore walnuts (or substitute regular walnuts) over salad.

Sprinkle with sea salt and freshly ground pepper.

Enjoy!

Layered Antipasto Salad Jars

A super simple spring and summer salad you will love to pack on all of your picnics.

Makes six 12-ounce salad jars

Make the balsamic dressing:

- ¼ cup balsamic vinegar
- ¼ cup olive oil
- 2 cloves garlic, minced
- Salt and freshly ground pepper, to taste

Whisk all balsamic dressing ingredients together until thoroughly mixed.

Assemble Layered Antipasto Salad Jars:

- 15 ounce can garbanzo beans, drained (you won't use the whole can)
- 1 cup hard salami, diced
- ¾ cup fresh mozzarella, diced
- 10.9 ounce jar marinated mushrooms with marinade
- ¼ cup fresh basil leaves, sliced into thin strips

Set up an assembly line with 12-ounce jars lined up on work surface.

Layer the antipasto salad in each jar in this order:

Bottom layer: an inch of garbanzo beans

Top with a drizzle of balsamic dressing.

Next layer: divide salami among jars.

Top with a drizzle of balsamic dressing.

Next later: divide marinated mushrooms among jars.

Top with a drizzle of balsamic dressing.

Next layer: divide cubed mozzarella among jars.

Top with a drizzle of balsamic dressing.

Top layer: Divide basil strips among jars.

Cover jars tightly with lids and refrigerate.

Store in cooler packed with ice for transport.

You may want to flip jars over or shake gently to distribute dressing before serving.

Enjoy!

Grilled Steak and Cherry Tomato Pasta Salad

Lovely to look at, even lovelier to eat, this steak pasta salad is a pleasure to prep ahead and have on hand!

Serves 4-6

- Two 6-ounce tenderloin steaks
- 1 cup cherry tomatoes, cut in half
- ½ cup walnuts
- 2 cups tri-color rotini, cooked according to package instructions, drained
- ½ cup blue cheese crumbles
- 1 tablespoon balsamic vinegar
- 1 ½ teaspoon olive oil
- 1/8 teaspoon salt
- 1/8 teaspoon freshly ground pepper
- 2 cups mixed greens, washed and dried
- Fresh thyme leaves, for garnish

Preheat barbecue grill to 350 degrees. Transfer steaks to preheated grill.

Season steaks on both sides with salt and freshly ground pepper. Cook steaks on grill for 7-8 minutes, for medium.

Turn steaks over and cook for an additional 7-8 minutes. Remove from grill and let rest. Brush a grill tray with olive oil and set on grill to preheat.

Transfer cherry tomatoes to preheated grill tray and grill briefly, 2-3 minutes.

Preheat oven to 300 degrees. Spread walnuts out on rimmed baking sheet.

Toast in preheated oven for 4-6 minutes, just until golden.

Whisk balsamic, olive oil and salt together until thoroughly combined.

Use a sharp knife to cut steak into bite-sized slices.

Toss together grilled steak, grilled tomatoes, cooked rotini pasta, blue cheese and dressing until well mixed. Cover and chill in refrigerator until ready to serve.

Line salad plates with a bed of mixed greens.

Top mixed greens with Grilled Steak and Tomato Pasta Salad.

Sprinkle each salad with toasted walnuts. Garnish salads with fresh thyme leaves.

Enjoy!

Baked Sweet Potato
with Garlic Roasted Vegetables

All you need is love…and maybe these garlic roasted vegetables tucked into a beautifully baked sweet potato.

Garlic Roasted Vegetables

- 1 yellow squash
- 1 small bunch asparagus, ends trimmed
- 4 small tomatoes
- 1 butternut squash
- 1 red bell pepper, seeded
- 2 cloves garlic, minced
- Kosher salt
- Freshly ground pepper
- ¼ cup extra virgin olive oil, divided

Preheat oven to 425 degrees.

Slice vegetables into ¼ inch thick slices of uniform length.

Brush large rimmed baking sheet with olive oil. Arrange sliced vegetables in a single layer to cover pan. Distribute minced garlic over sliced vegetables.

Drizzle with olive oil and sprinkle with salt and pepper.

Roast vegetables in preheated oven for 20-30 minutes until browned nicely.

Remove from oven and let cool.

Baked Sweet Potatoes with Garlic Roasted Vegetables

- 8 medium sweet potatoes
- 2 cups Garlic Roasted Vegetables, rewarmed, if desired
- 4 tablespoons butter with canola oil, divided

Preheat oven to 425 degrees.

Pierce top side of potatoes with a sharp knife or fork.

Bake sweet potatoes in preheated oven for 20-30 minutes, or until baked through.

Remove baked sweet potatoes from oven, split with a knife and stuff with Garlic Roasted Vegetables and butter with canola oil.

Serve hot.

Enjoy!

Sesame Slaw with Mushrooms, Broccoli and Almonds

It's love at first sweet and tangy bite with this satisfying, crunchy salad

Serves 4

Sesame Dressing

- ½ cup rice vinegar
- ¼ cup sugar
- ¼ tsp. salt
- ¼ cup sesame oil

Whisk all dressing ingredients in medium bowl until well-mixed.

Add to dressing in bowl:

- 2 cups angel hair cabbage
- 1 cup broccoli, thinly sliced
- 1 cup white mushrooms, thinly sliced
- 2 tbsp. slivered almonds
- 2 teaspoon toasted sesame seeds

Toss.

Serve.

Enjoy!

Prosciutto, Fig and Caramelized Onion Flatbread

You'll love this flatbread with its delicious layers of flavors.

Serves 4-6

- 2 tablespoons olive oil
- 1 medium sized sweet onion, sliced into thin rings
- 1 Italian Artisan pizza crust flatbread (grocery store bakery)
- ¼ cup confit of figs and balsamic vinegar
- ¼ pound prosciutto (deli), sliced into thin ribbons
- 4 ounces fresh mozzarella, sliced thinly (I used zesty marinated mozzarella which was delicious.)
- 1 tablespoon olive oil
- 1 tablespoon balsamic vinegar
- ¼ teaspoon. Kosher salt
- 1/8 teaspoon freshly ground pepper
- 2 cups baby arugula

Preheat oven to 400 degrees.

Heat 2 tablespoons olive oil in heavy pan over medium heat. Add onions and cook, stirring occasionally until softened.

When onions are softened, increase heat to medium high and cook, stirring frequently to prevent overbrowning, until caramelized. Remove from heat and let rest. (Can be made ahead and refrigerated.) Spread confit of figs and balsamic over flatbread crust to cover.

Top with prosciutto, caramelized onions and mozzarella slices, distributing evenly.

Bake in preheated oven for 12-14 minutes until cheese is melted and bubbly.

While flatbread is baking, dress the greens:

Whisk together 2 tablespoons olive oil and 1 tablespoons balsamic vinegar. Add salt and pepper and whisk to combine. Toss arugula with dressing and set aside.

Top baked flatbread with lightly dressed arugula. Slice into squares and serve.

Enjoy!

Company's Coming...Impress the Guests!

• •

Espresso-Chili Rubbed Pork Tenderloin • Chicken Cordon Bleu

Hoisin Glazed Seabass • Chicken Saltimbocca Lasagna

Mini Beef Wellingtons • The Napa Valley Nosher

Espresso-Chili Rubbed Pork Tenderloin

A sweet and spicy people-pleasing entrée to love.

Makes enough for one pork tenderloin, multiply quantities as needed.

- 1 teaspoon espresso powder

- 1 tablespoon. Kosher salt

- 1 tablespoon chili powder

- 2 tablespoons brown sugar

- ¼ teaspoon freshly ground pepper

Combine all ingredients in a mixing bowl.

Stir to mix.

Transfer to cutting board and roll pork tenderloin in rub to cover completely.

Grill rubbed pork on preheated grill (350 degrees) until cooked through, about 25 to 30 minutes.

Remove from grill and let rest briefly.

Slice and serve hot with grilled vegetables.

Enjoy!

Chicken Cordon Bleu

A lovely make-ahead entrée, fancy enough for guests, yet easy enough for anytime enjoyment.

Serves 4

- 2 large boneless skinless chicken breasts
- ¼ pound ham, thinly sliced
- ¼ pound Swiss cheese, thinly sliced
- 1 tablespoon butter
- 1 egg, beaten
- ¾ cup bread crumbs
- ½ cup grated parmesan cheese

Using a rolling pin, pound chicken breasts between sheets of waxed paper to a thickness of ¾ inch.

Cut each chicken breast in half lengthwise.

Layer ham over chicken portions, and then cheese.

Roll, being careful to keep ham and cheese tucked in, and secure with toothpicks.

Beat egg and place in shallow dish.

Place breadcrumbs in a second shallow dish.

Dip each chicken roll in egg to coat and roll in breadcrumbs to cover.

Brush baking dish with melted butter.

Place assembled chicken rolls in prepared baking dish. Cover and refrigerate until ready to bake.

Uncover and bake in preheated 350 degree oven for about 30 minutes, until baked through.

Serve with buttered rice.

Enjoy!

Hoisin Glazed Seabass on a Bed of Asian Sesame Slaw

You're sure to fall for this go-to dinner party dazzler~ hook, line and sinker!

Serves 4

Make the Asian Sesame Slaw

- ¼ cup sugar

- ¼ cup rice wine vinegar

- 2 tablespoons sesame oil

- 2 tablespoons real mayonnaise

- 5 ounces Angel Hair Cabbage Mix (finely shredded cabbage)

- ½ cup grated radish

- 1 tablespoon toasted sesame seeds (Asian foods aisle)

Combine sugar, vinegar, sesame oil and mayonnaise in medium mixing bowl and whisk to combine thoroughly. Add cabbage, grated radish and sesame seeds to the bowl and stir to combine. Cover and refrigerate until ready to serve.

Grill the Hoisin-glazed Sea Bass

(Thaw frozen sea bass fillets for several hours in refrigerator or under cold water in the sink before using. Pat dry.)

- 4 sea bass individual portions (6-ounce)

- 4 tablespoons butter, cut in 1 tablespoon pats

- 8-ounce jar hoisin sauce (Asian foods aisle), divided

- ¼ cup green onions, sliced thinly

Preheat grill to medium-high heat (about 400 degrees).

Lay out three sheets of aluminum foil on top of each other to cover large cutting board. Place the fillets in the center of the foil, leaving space in between. Fold all four sides of the foil into the center making a frame around the fillets, then bend sides up to make a tray.

Spoon 4 tablespoons hoisin sauce into small bowl. Using pastry brush, paint 1 tablespoon hoisin sauce over the top of each fillet. Put remaining hoisin sauce from jar in plastic baggie to garnish plates. Seal baggie.

Top each fillet with a pat of butter. Place foil tray with prepared fillets on preheated grill and grill for 6-7 minutes. The butter will melt and brown the edges of the fish. Do not overcook. The fish will continue to cook a bit after you remove it from the heat. Remove from grill. Tent with foil and let rest.

Make the Stir-Fried Sugar Snap Peas

- 2 6-ounce packages gourmet snap peas

- 2 tablespoons sesame oil

- Dash of salt

Fill a medium saucepan 2/3 full with water and bring to a boil. Add peapods, reduce heat and simmer for 4 minutes. Drain in colander and cover with ice cubes to stop cooking and set color.

Heat sesame oil in stir fry pan over medium high heat. Stir fry blanched snap peas briefly. Season with salt.

To plate:

Mound about ½ cup Asian Sesame Slaw in the center of each dinner plate. Set grilled sea bass fillet atop Asian Sesame Slaw. Sprinkle with sliced green onions. Arrange Stir-fried Sugar Snap Peas attractively around plate. Snip one corner of the baggie filled with reserved hoisin sauce and decorate rim of dinner plates.

Enjoy!

Chicken Saltimbocca Lasagna

Leave them longing for just one more bite of this fresh, fabulous twist on lasagna

Serves 12

- 2 tablespoons olive oil
- 2 pounds thickly sliced chicken breast (from the deli), cut in 1 inch cubes
- 2 cloves garlic, minced
- 2 cups Portobello mushrooms, chopped
- 2 teaspoons thyme
- 2 teaspoons oregano
- ½ teaspoon salt
- ¼ cup white wine
- 24-ounce jar Vodka sauce (pasta aisle)
- 2 cups Monterrey Jack cheese, grated
- ½ pound prosciutto, thinly sliced and cut into strips
- 1 9-ounce package no-cook lasagna noodle sheets
- Freshly snipped thyme

Preheat oven to 375 degrees.

Heat olive oil in a large sauté pan over medium high heat. Add garlic and mushrooms and cook until mushrooms are lightly browned.

Add thyme, oregano, salt, white wine and Vodka sauce. Simmer until reduced slightly, about 15 minutes.

Brush a 15 x 9-inch lasagna pan with olive oil.

Into the pan, layer:

- 1 cup sauce
- 4 sheets lasagna noodles
- grated cheese
- prosciutto strips

Continue layering until you have used all ingredients, ending with cheese and prosciutto strips. (At this point, you may cover and refrigerate until ready to bake if desired.)

Pour cream over and bake for about 40 minutes or until lightly browned.

Remove from oven and let set up for 10-15 minutes. Slice in squares and garnish with freshly snipped thyme.

Enjoy!

Mini Beef Wellingtons

Prepare to please with this elegant assemble-ahead classic.

- 17.3 ounce package frozen puff pastry, thawed according to package instructions

- 4 tablespoons butter, divided

- 8 ounce white mushrooms, finely chopped

- 2 tablespoons shallots, finely chopped

- ½ cup Dijon mustard

- 3 tablespoons fresh thyme sprigs, finely minced

- ½ teaspoon salt

- ½ teaspoon freshly ground pepper

- 10 small beef tenderloin portions, each 4 X 2 X 1 inch

- 1 egg, beaten

In a medium heavy saucepan, melt 2 tablespoons butter over medium high heat. Sauté shallots until soft. Add mushrooms and sauté briefly, about 2 minutes. Remove from heat.

Transfer mushroom mixture to small bowl and wipe out pan.

Return pan to heat. Add remaining 2 tablespoons butter to pan and melt.

Meanwhile, dip each tenderloin portion in Dijon, covering all sides.

Then dip in thyme/salt/pepper mixture to coat.

Sear tenderloin portions in heated butter, about 1 minute on each side, until lightly browned.

Transfer prepared tenderloins to baking pan, leaving room between each tenderloin.

Roll thawed pastry sheets out on lightly floured surface to 12 inch X 12 inch squares. (You will have two.)

Using a pizza cutter, cut puff pastry into 12 equal rectangles, large enough to drape over prepared tenderloins. (You may have to roll them out a bit more to make them big enough.)

Drape puff pastry pieces over tenderloins, tucking pastry and crimping to seal.

Brush beaten egg over pastry.

Use extra puff pastry to cut out stars.

Decorate each Wellington with puff pastry stars and brush with egg.

At this point, Mini Beef Wellingtons can be covered with foil and refrigerated until ready to bake and serve.

Remove from refrigerator, remove foil and let warm to room temperature before baking.

Preheat oven to 425 degrees.

Bake prepared Mini Beef Wellingtons in preheated oven for 10-12 minutes or until pastry is golden brown.

Serve immediately.

Enjoy!

The Napa Valley Nosher

Add this gourmet burger-to-love to your spring and summer entertaining lineup.

Makes six burgers

- 2 tablespoons Pinot Noir
- 2 pounds 80/20 ground chuck
- 1/2 teaspoon Kosher salt
- 1/4 teaspoon freshly ground pepper
- 1 tablespoon ice water

- 2 tablespoons Pinot Noir
- 1/2 cup real mayonnaise 1
- tablespoon shallots, finely minced
- 1 tablespoon butter

- 2 cups (packed) fresh baby arugula leaves
- 2 tablespoons olive oil
- 1/2 teaspoon Kosher salt
- 1/8 teaspoon. freshly ground pepper

- 5.3 ounces Cambozola (creamy triple cream soft cheese with blue veins)
- 1/2 cup flour
- 2 eggs, beaten
- 1/2 cup panko crumbs
- 12 Rhodes Texas sized rolls (freezer department of grocery store), thawed
- 1/4 cup butter
- 2 cloves garlic, minced

Using your hands, gently mix 2 tablespoons Sutter Home Pinot Noir, ground chuck, 1/2 teaspoon Kosher salt. 1/4 teaspoon freshly ground pepper and ice water just until incorporated. Divide into six equal parts and form round patties. Preheat barbecue grill to medium high heat.

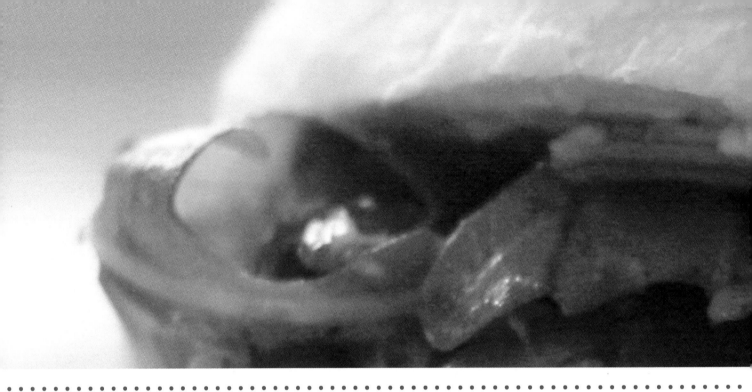

Heat butter in a medium sauté pan over medium high heat. Sauté shallots until softened. Combine 2 tablespoons. Pinot Noir, mayonnaise and sautéed shallots to make Pinot Shallot Spread.

Toss arugula with olive oil, salt and pepper.

Slice rind off of Cambozola and slice into six thin slices. Bread in flour, then beaten eggs, then panko to coat. Fry in hot peanut oil until golden on both sides, Transfer to paper towels.

Press two Texas sized rolls together and knead thoroughly until smooth to make each round bun and place on buttered baking sheet. Melt butter and garlic in microwave. Brush tops and sides of each bun with garlic butter. Bake in 350 degree oven for 16-18 minutes or until golden brown. Let cool slightly and slice in half horizontally.

Grill Pinot patties on preheated grill until they release easily, about 6 minutes, then cook other sides of Pinot patties until cooked through, another 6 minutes. Remove from grill and let rest briefly.

Spread insides of each Garlic Butter Bun with Pinot Shallot Spread. Top with grilled Pinot pattie, then Cambozola Croquette, then Lightly Dressed Arugula and top with Garlic Butter Bun.

Enjoy!

Desserts to Love and Die For!

• •

Basil-Balsamic Strawberries over Ice Cream • Mud Pie Babies

Salted Caramel Cashew Corn • Fresh Seasonal Berries with Crème Anglaise

Bittersweet Chocolate Mousse Cups

Pastry Wrapped Baked Apples with Almond Paste Filling

Basil-Balsamic Strawberries over Ice Cream

This simple spring dessert is a lovely grand finale to any dinner party.

Serves 4

- 2 cups fresh strawberries, sliced
- 3 tablespoons balsamic vinegar
- 1 ½ tablespoons brown sugar
- 3 tablespoons fresh basil leaves, cut into thin strips
- 1 pint French Vanilla Ice Cream

Heat vinegar and brown sugar over medium heat.

Simmer, stirring occasionally until sugar is dissolved and mixture is slightly thickened.

Add sliced strawberries and basil strips.

Remove from heat and set aside.

Serve Basil Balsamic Strawberries over French Vanilla Ice Cream.

Enjoy!

Mud Pie Babies

You'll love having these on hand in the freezer to serve throughout the summer season.

Makes about 20

- Two 2.25 ounce packages sliced almonds
- ¾ cup heavy cream
- 1 cup bittersweet chocolate chips
- 1 teaspoon almond extract
- ½ gallon coffee ice cream
- 9-ounce box Famous chocolate wafers (cookie aisle)

Toast almonds:

Preheat oven to 250 degrees.

Spread almonds out in a single layer on a baking sheet and toast for about 4 minutes or until golden brown.

Make Chocolate Almond Ganache:

Heat cream in a medium saucepan over medium heat until gently simmering.

Remove from heat. Add chocolate chips and almond extract and let sit briefly to allow chocolate chips to melt. Whisk until smooth. Set aside to cool.

Soften ice cream briefly.

Scoop 1 small scoop of ice cream on top of a single chocolate wafer.

Top with second chocolate wafer and press to spread ice cream out evenly. Use a table knife to remove excess ice cream and smooth the edges. Freeze briefly until firm. Repeat with additional chocolate wafers to use up wafers.

To assemble:

Dip one end of each frozen chocolate coffee ice cream sandwiches in Chocolate Almond Ganache and roll in toasted almonds. Set on tray and return to freezer. Repeat with remaining chocolate coffee ice cream sandwiches.

Enjoy!

(Wrap tightly in plastic wrap if you plan to keep them in the freezer for awhile.)

Salted Caramel Cashew Corn

Share the love by making a double recipe~ this tasty treat is highly addictive!

Makes an 11 by 18 inch pan

- 1 bag microwave popcorn
- 1 cup butter
- 2 cups brown sugar
- ½ cup light corn syrup
- 1 teaspoon Kosher salt
- ½ teaspoon. baking soda
- 1 teaspoon vanilla extract
- 1 cup cashew pieces

Pop the microwave popcorn, according to package instructions.

Preheat oven to 250 degrees.

Heat butter, brown sugar, light corn syrup and salt in a heavy medium saucepan over medium high heat until butter melts, stirring occasionally. Bring to a boil and boil for 5 minutes.

Remove from heat and add baking soda and vanilla, stirring to incorporate.

Pour salted caramel syrup over popped corn in large mixing bowl.

Stir to distribute.

Spread onto large rimmed baking sheet and bake, stirring once every 15 minutes, for a total of 30 minutes to distribute Salted Caramel Syrup.

Remove from oven, sprinkle with cashews, stir, and spread out on parchment paper and let cool.

Break into bite-sized clusters.

Enjoy!

Fresh Seasonal Berries with Crème Anglaise

A lovely way to serve up fresh, seasonal berries.

Serves 4-6

- 1 pint fresh raspberries
- 1 pint fresh blueberries
- 1 pint fresh strawberries, hulled and cut into small pieces
- Fresh mint sprigs, for garnish
- ¼ cup white chocolate grated with microplane
- 2 cups heavy cream
- ¼ teaspoon Kosher salt
- 1 vanilla bean
- 1/3 cup sugar
- 5 egg yolks

Crème Anglaise:

Using the tip of a sharp paring knife, split vanilla bean down the center to expose tiny vanilla seeds. Heat cream, vanilla bean and salt over medium heat, stirring occasionally just until it looks like it is going to simmer.

Whisk egg yolks and sugar together until well mixed.

Remove from heat and whisk egg yolk mixture into cream until blended.

Return to heat, stirring constantly until thickened, reducing heat slightly if necessary to prevent from simmering.

Continue cooking until mixture has thickened enough to coat the back of a wooden spoon.

Remove from heat and let cool slightly.

Strain into a clean glass bowl.

Cool to room temperature.

Cover and chill until ready to serve.

To serve:

Combine berries in bowl and stir to mix.

Distribute berries among glass goblets or other dessert dishes.

Ladle Crème Anglaise over the berries.

Top with grated white chocolate and mint sprigs.

Enjoy!

Melt-in-your-Mouth
Chocolate
Mousse Cups

Because let's face it, chocolate is love.

Makes 12 mousse cups

*Note: Start the recipe at least the day before you plan to serve it as the mousse mixture require overnight chilling before beating.

- Two 10-ounce bags Ghiradelli (or other higher quality) bittersweet chocolate chips

- 1 quart heavy whipping cream

- 12 ounces Ghiradelli (or other higher quality) bittersweet chocolate chips

- 2 teaspoons pure almond extract

- ¼ teaspoon Kosher salt

- 12 foil cupcake liners

1. Melt 2- 10 ounce bags chocolate in medium sized glass bowl in the microwave. Stir until smooth.

2. Dip each foil cupcake liner into the melted chocolate to coat outside and set on foil-lined tray. Set in freezer to cool, then repeat dipping process one more time to reinforce thickness of chocolate cups. Return chocolate cups to freezer to chill until ready to fill.

3. Pipe 12 chocolate hearts onto a foil-lined tray, using leftover melted chocolate.

Chill in freezer until ready to garnish chocolate mousse cups.

4. Heat cream in microwave until hot. Then add 12 ounces chocolate, whisk until smooth.

5. Cover and chill chocolate mousse mixture in refrigerator overnight.

6. Beat chocolate mousse mixture until thickened but not stiff.

7. Peel foil liners out of chocolate cups, being careful, as they are fragile.

8. Pipe chocolate mousse into chocolate cups.

9. Garnish with chocolate hearts and serve.

Enjoy!

Pastry Wrapped Baked Apples
with Almond Paste Filling

If you love apple pie, you'll go head over heels for these baked apple beauties.

Makes 4

Poach apples:

∙∙∙∙∙∙∙∙∙∙∙∙∙∙∙∙∙∙∙∙∙∙∙∙∙∙∙∙∙∙∙∙∙∙∙

- 4 small honeycrisp or gala apples, peeled
- 4 cups water
- Juice of 1 lemon
- ½ cup sugar

Combine water, lemon juice and sugar in sauce pan big enough to fit apples over medium heat.Stir to combine.

Set apples upright in poaching liquid.

Bring to a simmer and poach apples for 15 minutes.

Remove from heat and transfer poached apples to cutting board. Let cool.

Cut a thin slice off the bottom of each apple to make it stand upright.

Remove core with seeds from each apple.

Fill apples:

∙∙∙∙∙∙∙∙∙∙∙∙∙∙∙∙∙∙∙∙∙∙∙∙∙∙∙∙∙∙∙∙∙∙∙

- 7 ounce package almond paste
- ½ cup sliced almonds
- 2 tablespoons butter, softened
- ½ teaspoon almond extract
- 2 tablespoons sugar

Combine all ingredients in bowl of electric mixer. Beat ingredients until well-mixed. Fill poached apples will filling.

Wrap apples:

∙∙∙∙∙∙∙∙∙∙∙∙∙∙∙∙∙∙∙∙∙∙∙∙∙∙∙∙∙∙∙∙∙∙∙

- 17.3 ounce package puff pastry, thawed
- ¼ cup melted butter
- ¼ cup sliced almonds

Preheat oven to 375 degrees. Set oven rack in upper middle of oven.

Unfold and lay out puff pastry sheets on work surface. Brush pastry sheets with melted butter and sprinkle with almond slices. Use a rolling pin to press almond slices into puff pastry.

Cut puff pastry into thin strips, about ½ inch thick. Butter rimmed baking sheet.

Start at bottom of each poached filled apple and carefully wrap a pastry strip all the way around each apple, working your way up to the top of the apple.

Press strips to adhere to apples. Transfer pastry-wrapped apples to buttered baking sheet, leaving space in between apples.

Bake apples in preheated oven for about 18 minutes, or until pastry is lightly browned. Serve hot.

Enjoy!

Little Book
Big Thanks

Thank you to~

Mom, for sharing your love of cooking with me from the very beginning.

Dad, for your constant encouragement and praise.

Mike, for being my number one fan.

Mackenzie and Madison, for making me so proud and nudging me along to get better every day.

Tyler and Kelly, for your brotherly love always.

Karen and Tom, for taste-testing and loving so many contest entries along the way.

Jamie, for stirring up so much support for so long.

Tim, for reminding me that I am exactly where I need to be, doing exactly what I need to be doing.

Anne, for pointing out that "Rome wasn't built in a day" and continuing to ask me, "What's next?" and editing my cookbook!

Marnie, for showing me through your shining example that there is no dress rehearsal and encouraging me to do it now.

Jenny, for creating the beautiful endpapers for the book!

And everyone else who chatted me up at a party, stopped me in the grocery store, or shot me an email or Facebook message to convince me to write a cookbook.

Elizabeth Gilbert, my hero, for Big Magic and all of your sage advice.

Ann Patchett, for sharing The Getaway Car, exactly what I needed to read before diving in.

WHAT A WONDERFUL WAY TO START THE DAY

FAST, FRESH AND FABULOUS

COMPANY'S COMING...
IMPRESS THE GUESTS

DESSERTS TO LOVE AND DIE FOR